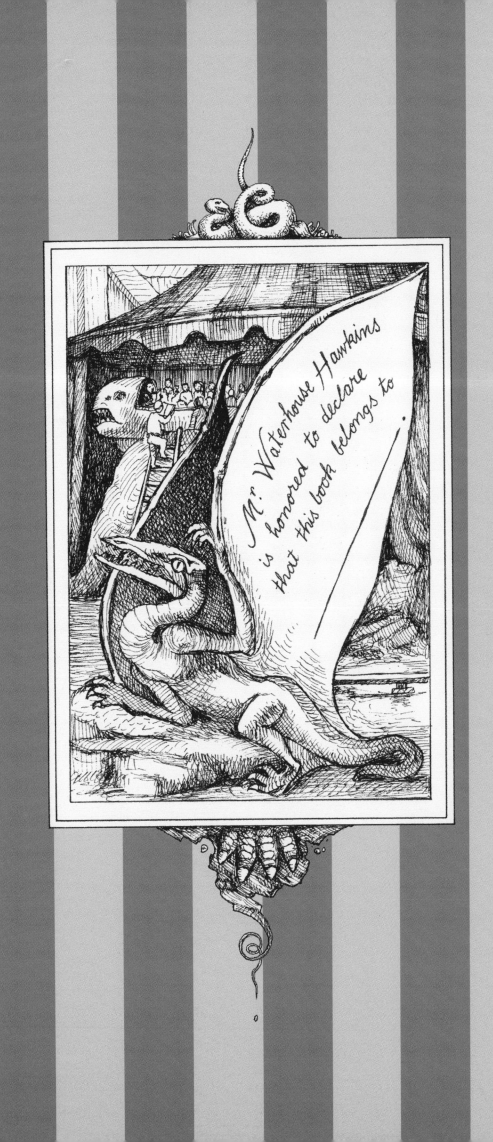

Mr. Waterhouse Hawkins is honored to declare that this book belongs to

WELCOME TO

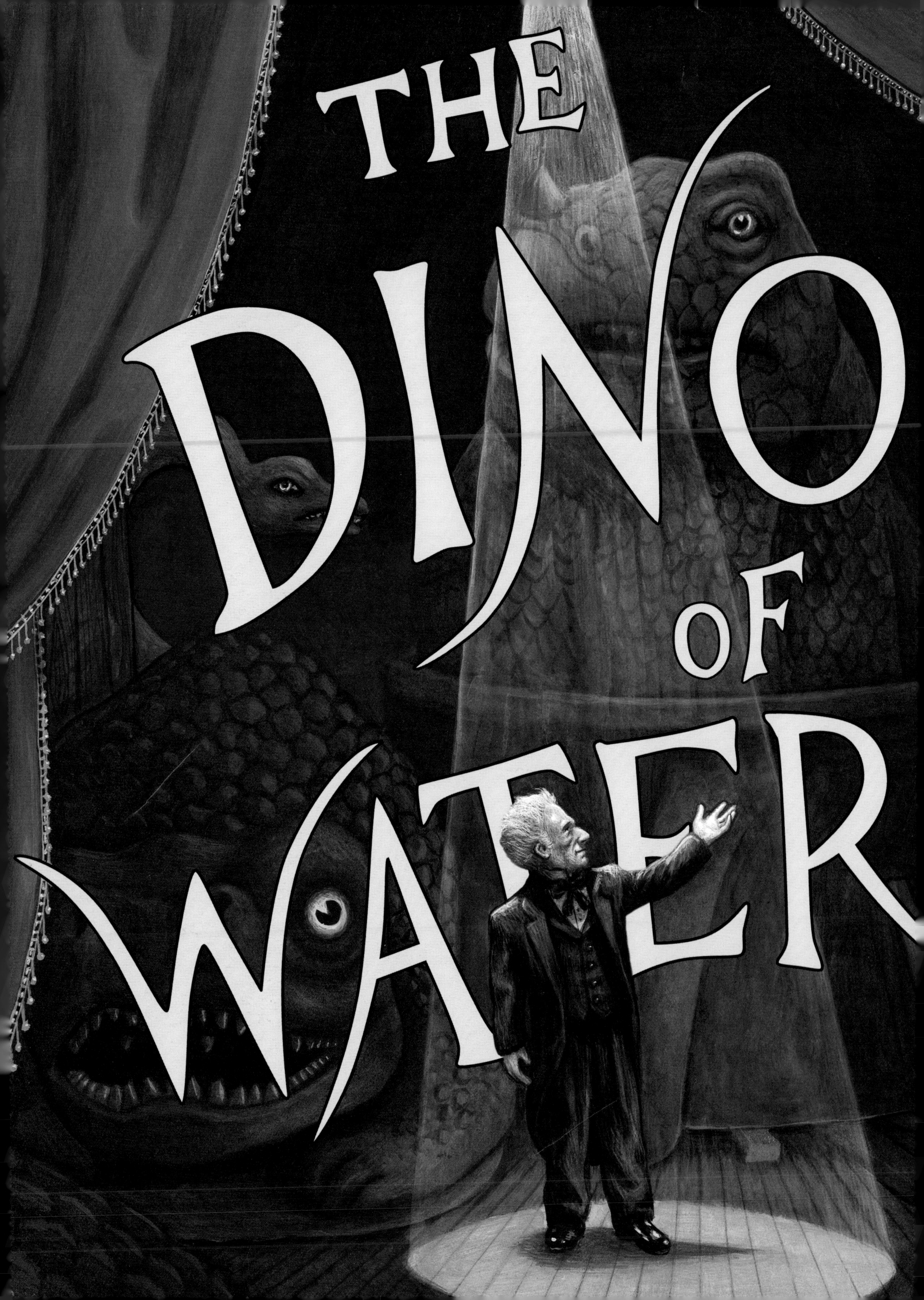
THE
DINO
OF
WATER

SAURS

HOUSE

HAWKINS

For Mary, Ellen, Tasha, and Kim.
With special thanks to:
Tracy Mack, for helping me find the story *in history;*
and Brian Selznick, for bringing this story to life. —B. K.

For Steve McCarthy —B. S.

The AUTHOR and the ARTIST gratefully acknowledge: IN ENGLAND, Sandra Chapman, Lorraine Cornish, Rachel Farmer, Melanie Lawes, and Ann Lum of the Natural History Museum in London; Melvyn Harrison and Anne Roy at the Crystal Palace Foundation; Ray Sacks from the Crystal Palace Campaign; and Nicola Lee at the Crystal Palace Park (for taking Brian onto Dinosaur Island). IN AMERICA, Carol Spawn of The Academy of Natural Sciences in Philadelphia; Matthew Miles at the Humboldt County Library in California; Jed Lackritz of the New York City Department of Parks and Recreation and Sister Rita King from the Sisters of Charity in the Bronx; Maureen McCormick at Princeton University; and Mick Gilbert and Steve McCarthy for their book *The Crystal Palace Dinosaurs*, and especially to Steve for fact-checking this book and for all his help and insights.

Out of over 40 references, the following were especially helpful in creating this book: Adrian Desmond's *The Hot-Blooded Dinosaurs* and his article, "Central Park's Fragile Dinosaurs" in *Natural History*; Donald F. Glut's *The Dinosaur Scrapbook*; William A. Sarjeant's article, "Crystal Palace," in *Encyclopedia of Dinosaurs*; and most importantly, Steve McCarthy's *The Crystal Palace Dinosaurs: The Story of the World's First Prehistoric Sculptures*. We also relied heavily on articles in the following primary sources: *The Illustrated London News* (1853 – 1854); *The London Quarterly Review* (1854); *The New York Times* (1868 – 1872); and last, but most certainly not least, B. Waterhouse Hawkins' article, "On Visual Education as Applied to Geology," in *Journal of the Society of Arts* (1854).

This book was originally published in hardcover by Scholastic Press in 2001.

ISBN-13: 978-0-439-11495-0
ISBN-10: 0-439-11495-0

12 11 10 9 8 7 6 5 4 3 2   10 11 12 13 14/0

Printed in the U.S.A.   08
This edition first printing, March 2009

The text type was set in 12-point Hoefler Text. The display type was set in Sign Painter's DeVinne, and Hoefler Engraved. Handlettering throughout was drawn by Brian Selznick. The menu facsimile on page 54 is reproduced courtesy of the Ewell Sale Stewart Library, The Academy of Natural Sciences in Philadelphia. Book design by Brian Selznick and David Saylor.

SCHOLASTIC INC.
New York Toronto London Auckland Sydney Mexico City New Delhi Hong Kong Buenos Aires

THE DINOSAURS OF WATERHOUSE HAWKINS

AN ILLUMINATING HISTORY OF MR. WATERHOUSE HAWKINS,

ARTIST AND LECTURER

By

BARBARA KERLEY

With drawings by

BRIAN SELZNICK

Many of which are based on the

original sketches of Mr. Hawkins

A TRUE DINOSAUR STORY
— IN THREE AGES —

FROM A CHILDHOOD LOVE OF ART, TO THE

MONUMENTAL DINOSAUR SCULPTURES AT THE

CRYSTAL PALACE IN ENGLAND, TO THE THWARTED

WORK IN NEW YORK'S CENTRAL PARK . . .

IT'S ALL HERE!

HORSE-DRAWN carriages clattered down the streets of London in 1853. Gentlemen tipped their hats to ladies passing by. Children ducked and dodged on their way to school.

But Benjamin Waterhouse Hawkins had no time to be out and about. Waterhouse, as he liked to call himself, hurried toward his workshop in a park south of town. He was expecting some very important visitors. He didn't want to be late.

As he neared his workshop, Waterhouse thought of the hours he'd spent outside as a boy. Like many artists, he had grown up sketching the world around him. By the time he was a young man, he'd found his true passion: animals. He loved to draw and paint them. But what he really loved was sculpting models of them. Through his care and hard work, they seemed to come to life.

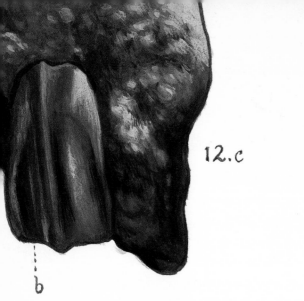

12.c

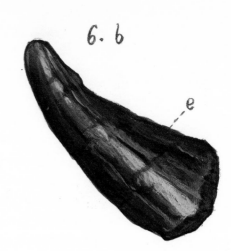

6. b

6.c

——————

Now Waterhouse was busy with a most exciting project: He was building dinosaurs! His creations would prowl the grounds of Queen Victoria and Prince Albert's new art and science museum, the Crystal Palace.

Even though the English had found the first known dinosaur fossil many years before — and the bones of more dinosaurs had been unearthed in England since then — in 1853, most people had no idea what a dinosaur looked like.

Scientists weren't sure either, for the only fossils were some bits and pieces — a tooth here, a bone there. But they thought that if they studied a fossil and compared it to a living animal, they could fill in the blanks.

And so, with the help of scientist Richard Owen, who checked every muscle, bone, and spike, that's exactly what Waterhouse was doing. He wanted to create such perfect models that anyone — a crowd of curious children, England's leading scientists, even the Queen herself! — could gaze at his dinosaurs and see into the past.

——————

4. a

6 e

3. b

c

2. a

e

3. a

a

9

b

2. b

e

b

7

2. c

a

Iguanodon

Iguana

Iguanodon Teeth

Megalosaurus

7. a

Waterhouse threw open the doors to his workshop. Nervously, he tidied up here and there. His assistants came, then Richard Owen.

At last, the visitors arrived: Queen Victoria and Prince Albert!

The Queen's eyes grew wide in surprise. Waterhouse's creatures were extraordinary! How on earth had he made them?

He was happy to explain: The iguanodon, for instance, had teeth that were quite similar to the teeth of an iguana. The iguanodon, then, must surely have looked like a giant iguana. Waterhouse pointed out that the few iguanodon bones helped determine the model's size and proportion. And another bone — almost a spike — most likely sat on the nose, like a rhino's horn.

Just so for the megalosaurus. Start with its jawbone. Compare it to the anatomy of a lizard. Fill in the blanks. And voilà! A dinosaur more than forty feet long.

Waterhouse was also making ancient reptiles and amphibians. While Richard Owen could imagine their shapes, it took an artist to bring the animals to life.

Designing the creatures was only the first step. There was still the monumental task of building them.

Waterhouse showed his guests the small models he'd made, correct in every detail, from scales on the nose to nails on the toes. With the help of his assistants, he had formed the life-size clay figures and created the molds from them. Then he erected iron skeletons, built brick foundations, and covered the whole thing with cement casts from the dinosaur-shaped molds.

"It is no less," Waterhouse concluded, "than building a house upon four columns."

In the weeks to follow, Waterhouse basked in the glow of the Queen's approval. But he would soon face a much tougher set of critics: England's leading scientists. Waterhouse wanted to be accepted into this circle of eminent men. What would they think of his dinosaurs?

There was only one way to find out. Waterhouse would show them. But why not do it with a little style?

A dinner party. On New Year's Eve, no less. And not just any dinner party. Waterhouse would stage an event that no one would ever forget!

He sketched twenty-one invitations to the top scientists and supporters of the day, the words inscribed on a drawing of a pterodactyl wing. He pored over menus with the caterer.

The iguanodon mold was hauled outside. A platform was built. A tent erected.

As the hour drew near, the table was elegantly set, and names of famous scientists — the fathers of paleontology — were strung above the tent walls. All was ready.

With great anticipation, Waterhouse dressed for the occasion in his finest attire. He was ready to reveal his masterpiece!

When the guests arrived, they gasped with delight!

Waterhouse smiled as he signaled for dinner to begin. With solemn formality, the footmen served course after course from silver platters. Up and down the steps of the platform they carried the lavish feast: rabbit soup, fish, ham, and even pigeon pie. For dessert, there were nuts, pastries, pudding, and plums. Two footmen stayed busy simply pouring the wines.

For eight hours, the men rang in the New Year. They laughed and shouted. They made speech after speech, toasting Waterhouse Hawkins. All the guests agreed: The iguanodon was a marvelous success. By midnight they were belting out a song created especially for the occasion:

THE JOLLY OLD BEAST IS NOT DECEASED

THERE'S LIFE IN HIM AGAIN!

The next months passed by in concrete, stone, and iron, as Waterhouse put the finishing touches on his dinosaurs. Inside the iguanodon's lower jaw he signed the work: B. HAWKINS, BUILDER, 1854. The models were now ready for the grand opening of the Crystal Palace at Sydenham Park.

Forty thousand spectators attended the regal ceremony. In the sun-filled center court, Waterhouse mingled with scientists and foreign dignitaries. At last, the Queen arrived! The crowd cheered, "Hurrah!"

Cannons boomed, music swelled, and a choir of one thousand voices sang. Waterhouse bowed before the Queen. Then she and Prince Albert invited the spectators to enjoy the amazing sights.

Waterhouse hurried to the lake and waited for the crowd to arrive.

First two, then ten, then a dozen more . . . Gasped! Shrieked! Laughed and cried: So this was a dinosaur!

Waterhouse was thrilled. For in addition to being an artist, he also saw himself as a teacher. He was convinced that the best way for people to learn about something was to see it. With this love of art and teaching, he knew he could do more. Educational posters. Small models anyone could buy. Lectures. Books to illustrate. For the next fourteen years, Waterhouse did it all.

News of his success had reached America. In 1868, Waterhouse traveled to New York City, filling a lecture hall for talks about dinosaurs, evolution, even dragons. As he spoke, he sketched such marvelous illustrations that the audience burst into applause.

And then, Waterhouse received a delightful surprise: a letter from the head of Central Park, inviting him to build American dinosaurs! His models would inhabit a museum planned for the park's southwest corner.

Waterhouse was excited. America's first two dinosaurs, Hadrosaurus and Laelaps, had only recently been discovered. Here was his chance to bring these dinosaurs to life for all to see.

WATERHOUSE set right to work. He spent the next six months traveling to American museums to learn about American dinosaurs. Again, he built something no one had ever seen before: the first model of a complete dinosaur skeleton.

He presented the Hadrosaurus to The Academy of Natural Sciences in Philadelphia, where it was welcomed with great enthusiasm.

Now Waterhouse was ready to build his dinosaurs. He returned to New York City to the workshop built for him in Central Park. He hired an assistant, and the real work began. Small models. Life-size clay figures. Iron skeletons. Dinosaurs.

While he and his assistant toiled inside, workmen outside began building the museum. Like the Crystal Palace, the Paleozoic Museum would be an enormous structure of iron and glass with a beautiful arched ceiling.

Day after day, workmen dug the foundation.

Then disaster struck. William "Boss" Tweed, a corrupt politician who controlled much of New York City, said the museum was a waste of money. At six feet tall and three hundred pounds, Boss Tweed was a big man, with an even bigger thirst for power. He reorganized the Parks Department and put his own men in charge. Waterhouse watched in dismay as work on the museum was stopped.

He began looking for a new home for his dinosaurs. But he was frustrated that a thieving scoundrel could thwart almost two years of work.

In March of 1871, Waterhouse gave a speech at the New York Lyceum of Natural History. He stressed the importance of science and art, then shared the troubles he'd had with the Boss.

"I trust, however," Waterhouse concluded, "that in time the good sense of the people will awaken and that they will realize the vast importance of my work."

The audience agreed. One man called the Boss greedy. Another said that the Boss was an "Enemy of Mankind." *The New York Times* printed it all.

Waterhouse carried on with his work, but on May 3, his dream was shattered.

Vandals broke into his workshop. Wielding sledgehammers, they smashed the dinosaurs. Then they carted the pieces outside and buried them in the park.

Waterhouse arrived to find chaos: chunks of rubble, mangled wire, plaster shards, and dust. He simply couldn't believe it.

Waterhouse stumbled outside, only to find mounds of dirt and dinosaur rubble. Two years of his life, utterly ruined.

This could only be the work of Boss Tweed. The more Waterhouse thought about it, the angrier he became. He protested to the Parks Department. The situation was outrageous! Criminal! Surely something could be done!

But Waterhouse was bluntly told not to waste his time with "dead animals" when there were so many living ones around.

Waterhouse staggered away. His dinosaurs were broken, and so was his spirit.

But in spite of the Boss, Waterhouse would give America her dinosaurs.

He left New York to create towering hadrosaur skeletons for Princeton University in New Jersey and the Smithsonian Institute in Washington, D. C. He stayed on at Princeton, yet again creating something that no one had ever seen before: the first series of paintings showing the development of life on Earth, including his beloved dinosaurs.

Waterhouse was now seventy-one years old. It was time to go home.

WATERHOUSE returned to London and exciting news: Thirty iguanodon skeletons had been discovered in a coal mine in Belgium. It now appeared that Waterhouse's beloved iguanodon might have walked upright, on its hind feet. And the spike on the nose — like a rhino's horn — might actually be a thumb. Imagine that!

Waterhouse settled back into his cottage, Fossil Villa, near the Crystal Palace. And on pleasant afternoons, as he walked to the park and his marvelous creations, he wondered: What other surprises would scientists dig up as they searched the world for dinosaurs?

Just as he had hoped, his models were the start of something wonderful: the world's first encounter with these ancient animals.

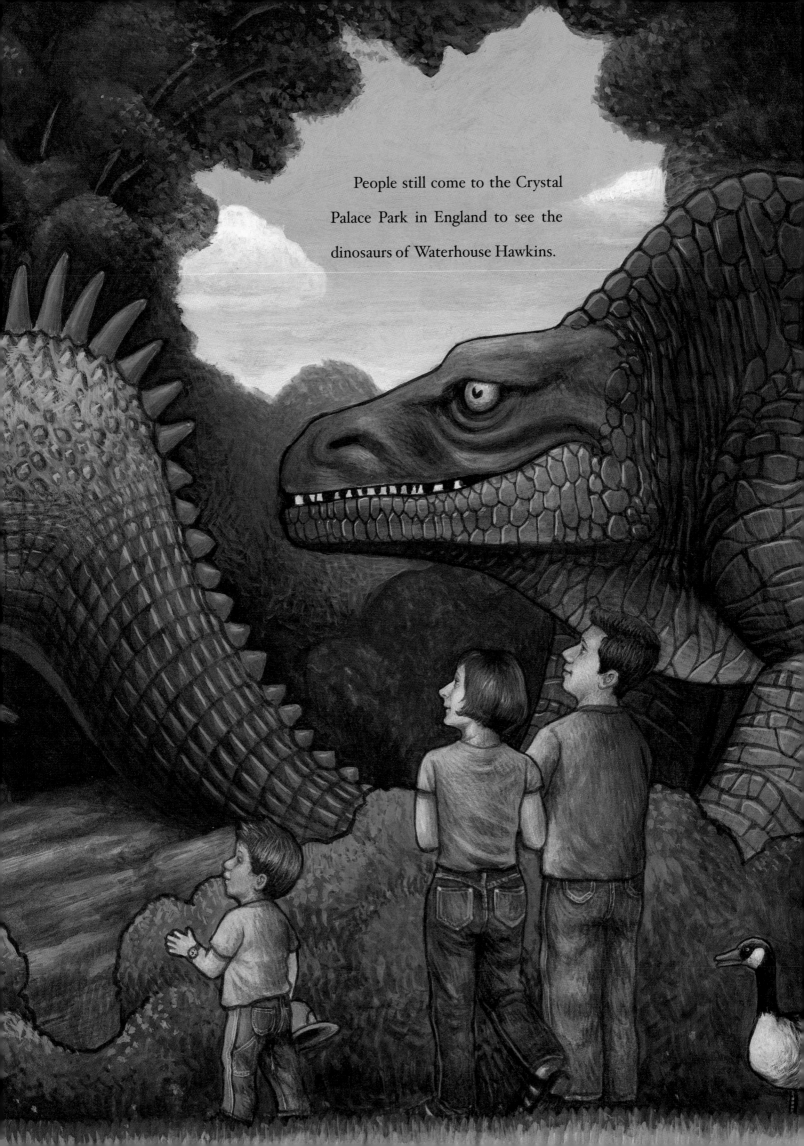

People still come to the Crystal
Palace Park in England to see the
dinosaurs of Waterhouse Hawkins.

And while his

American dinosaurs

no longer stand,

somewhere,

buried in Central Park,

pieces of his dinosaurs

remain.

AUTHOR'S NOTE

What first drew me to this story, of course, was the dinner party. That and the wonderful name, Waterhouse Hawkins. I remember flipping through a dinosaur book one day in 1996 when I first saw the picture: the ever-so-formal waiters, the candlesticks, the chandelier, and all those elegant gentlemen stuffed into that incredible dinosaur. What was the story behind this picture?

I've always been fascinated by artists, inventors, and creative people who stretch the boundaries of what's been done before. Waterhouse did this in a monumental way. Dinosaurs are such a part of our lives now that we're not surprised to hear a small child rattle off those long, long names. But there was a time when no one, besides a handful of scientists, knew what a dinosaur was. Waterhouse changed that.

THE MODELS

We now know that many of Waterhouse's models are inaccurate. Megalosaurus, for instance, walked on two feet, not four. Scientists now think Hylaeosaurus had spikes running from shoulder to hip instead of down the spine. Dicynodon had no shell. Labyrinthodon looked more like a crocodile than a frog. And the famous Iguanodon had no spike on its head, but instead two spiked thumbs.

But the fact that new fossil discoveries, which came fast and furious in the last years of Waterhouse's life, showed the models to be inaccurate doesn't make them any less valuable. Waterhouse's models are what first got people excited about dinosaurs. We're still excited, 150 years later.

As for how the models were designed—by filling in the blanks—Richard Owen, the renowned scientist who supervised the project, was famous for it. He once correctly predicted the structure of an entire bird by studying a single leg bone. Richard Owen was viewed as the top comparative anatomist in England in the mid-nineteenth century. In fact, he created the word "dinosaur." But while Richard Owen provided guidance, it was Waterhouse who actually sculpted the missing bones. He pioneered the technique that is still being used today.

It's not clear who first suggested that the models be built. Some historians say Richard Owen. Others say Queen Victoria's husband, Prince Albert. But once hired, Waterhouse dove right in and made the project his own.

Working together, he and Richard Owen designed each creature. Then Waterhouse—using stone, wire, clay, and cement—captured not just the creature's size and shape, but its spirit. Almost every account of his "unique, arduous, and successful undertaking," as Waterhouse later described it, talks about how hard he worked. Every day, whatever the weather, he slogged across the muddy field at Sydenham Park to stand in a cold, drafty building and work: 30 tons of clay, 600 bricks, 1500 tiles, 38 casks of cement, 90 casks of broken stone, iron columns 7 inches thick, and 100 feet of iron hooping. All this, to build one iguanodon!

THE SPIRIT OF THE ARTIST

So little has been written about Waterhouse's personal life that at times when researching this book, I felt a bit like Richard Owen, holding a single leg bone and trying to guess the bird. I was thrilled to find a few samples of Waterhouse's writings and several newspaper articles recounting his speeches. From these sources, I drew quotes for the book.

We do know that Waterhouse was born in London in 1807. He studied painting and sculpture, and by the time he was twenty, concentrated on natural history. He exhibited paintings in several London galleries and even helped illustrate Charles Darwin's *The Zoology of the Voyage of HMS* Beagle. By 1842, he was making animal models. He wrote several books on animal anatomy and, after his Crystal Palace success, became one of England's most popular illustrators of natural history books.

It's also clear that he was extraordinarily devoted to his work. In February of 1870, *The New York Times* published an article with a wonderful description of Waterhouse, who, at sixty-three years old, was hard at work building the Central Park dinosaurs: "In stature he is about five feet eight inches, of an active, energetic temperament, vigorous for his years, enthusiastic in all that pertains to his work, a hard student, and, notwithstanding he has already devoted a lifetime to research, he is still active in the pursuit of knowledge."

Reports of his lectures also reveal his great sense of showmanship. Newspaper articles mention "the illustrations on the blackboard, which were made with a rapidity and accuracy at once amusing and astonishing. . . . one of those entertainments that must be seen to be appreciated."

Waterhouse had a flair for the dramatic. In a paper he read before the Society of Arts in 1854 (published that same year in the *Journal of the Society of Arts*) he described the Crystal Palace models as "vast forms and gigantic beasts. . .called up from the abyss of time and from the depths of the earth."

And there is a wonderful mix of humility and pride evident in his acceptance of the invitation to build the Central Park dinosaurs:

> . . . *I came among you a stranger scarcely expecting to resume my former labors . . . in those subjects to which I have devoted my life. . . . I am prepared to enter at once upon . . . the undertaking.*
> *With the highest consideration,*
> *I am, dear Sir,*
> *Yours, faithfully,* B. Waterhouse Hawkins

True to his word, Waterhouse set right to work on his Central Park dinosaurs — Hadrosaurus and Laelaps (which is now known as Dryptosaurus) plus other ancient animals such as the Mastodon and the giant ground sloth, Megatherium. He began work in the Arsenal Building and then moved the project to a "temporary shed" about a year later. It was in this shed that Tweed's vandals wreaked their carnage.

THE BOSS

"Boss" Tweed was one of the most corrupt politicians America has ever seen. He stole money from city budgets and gave many people jobs in exchange for their support. But exactly why did he want the Central Park dinosaurs smashed? Even if they were a waste of money, as Tweed claimed, why destroy what Waterhouse had already built?

A likely explanation is that Waterhouse's speech — and the audience's reaction—were seen by Tweed as a challenge to his authority. Just a few weeks after Waterhouse's dinosaurs were destroyed, Tweed was arrested for fraud and theft. He escaped to Spain but was recaptured and sent back to New York. He later died in prison.

A year after Waterhouse's models were demolished, *The New York Times* reported that some of the fragments were dug up, but "in thousands of pieces" and beyond repair. To this day, the rest remain buried in Central Park, their exact location unknown.

It's not surprising that Waterhouse was infuriated by Tweed's destruction of the models and remained bitter about it for years. But the fact that Waterhouse was able to put the loss behind him and continue his work demonstrates better than anything his determination and dedication.

THE PALACE

The Crystal Palace was the first large iron-framed glass building ever made, with almost 300,000 panes of glass. The pieces all bolted together. The design was so new, however, that many people were convinced the building would collapse. Before it was opened to the public, squads of soldiers stomped around inside to prove that the building wouldn't come crashing down.

It was originally built in Hyde Park, London, to house the first world's fair, the Great Exhibition of 1851. After the exhibition closed, the building was dismantled, enlarged, and re-erected in Sydenham to serve as a museum of the arts and sciences. It was for this grand reopening that Waterhouse built his dinosaurs.

For the next eighty-two years, millions of people visited the Palace to enjoy concerts, firework displays, and the incredible exhibits.

The Crystal Palace burned to the ground in 1936. Luckily, Waterhouse's dinosaurs were spared from the flames. They stand in Sydenham today.

ILLUSTRATOR'S NOTE

Maybe it was because I love to build models or because I've always been fascinated by dinosaurs and cannot resist a good mystery, but from the moment I first learned about Waterhouse Hawkins, I was hooked.

I began my research at The Academy of Natural Sciences in Philadelphia, where Barbara Kerley had heard there was a rare scrapbook—which Waterhouse Hawkins himself may have put together. It was filled with photographs and many of his original drawings. Apparently, a family in Virginia had owned the scrapbook for years, never knowing where it came from or how they got it. The kids in the family called it "The Dinosaur Book," and from the state of its pages, one can tell that they must have loved it very much. When the kids grew up, their parents were going to sell the book at a garage sale for fifty cents. Luckily, a neighbor spotted its possible importance, and it made its way to Philadelphia. To this day, it is the single best primary source of Waterhouse material.

In a small room in the basement, the archivist, Carol Spawn, presented me with a box that contained the scrapbook. Because it was well over a hundred years old and made of leather, the pages had been removed and placed in protective sleeves to guard against further wear. With trembling hands, I leafed through the original photographs and drawings. Many of my illustrations (as well as the red and black borders) are based on what I found in the scrapbook. The scrapbook also contained one of the original invitations to the Iguanodon dinner, which became, with a few changes, the bookplate on the front endpaper. The book jacket is inspired by the cover of the leather scrapbook, with the hope that our book would have some of the quality of the Dinosaur Book that those kids had grown up with in Virginia.

Now the real fun began. I had to go to England to see Waterhouse's dinosaurs for myself! I arrived at the Crystal Palace Park in Sydenham after a light rainfall. Nicola Bailey, a park ranger, led me through the park, into an abandoned children's zoo, through a locked gate, across a small waterfall (guarded by two very mean geese), and finally, onto Dinosaur Island, which is generally closed to the public. There they were! The dinosaurs loomed larger and more magnificent than I could have ever imagined. It was like stepping back in time.

I was given the key to the gate so I could come and go as I pleased, and for three days I sketched and photographed the dinosaurs. I even managed to climb up into the Iguanodon, where I stood amid the bricks and iron supports, dizzy with excitement. One hundred and forty-six years earlier, Waterhouse had hosted his dinner party inside the mold of this very dinosaur!

On my last day with the dinosaurs, one of the geese bit me, so I put him in the book. I finished up my time in England with research at the Natural History Museum in London, where Waterhouse had also done some work. There I saw more folders filled with his original drawings and lithographs.

Everything you see in the pictures for this book is based on my research and Barbara's. The only exception is the outline for the Paleozoic museum proposed for Central Park. There are no known sketches of the exterior of the building, so I had to extrapolate from the few surviving sketches of its interior.

I had never heard about Waterhouse Hawkins before I began work on this book, but suddenly he became the center of my life. I hope you've enjoyed learning about him and his dinosaurs as much as I have.

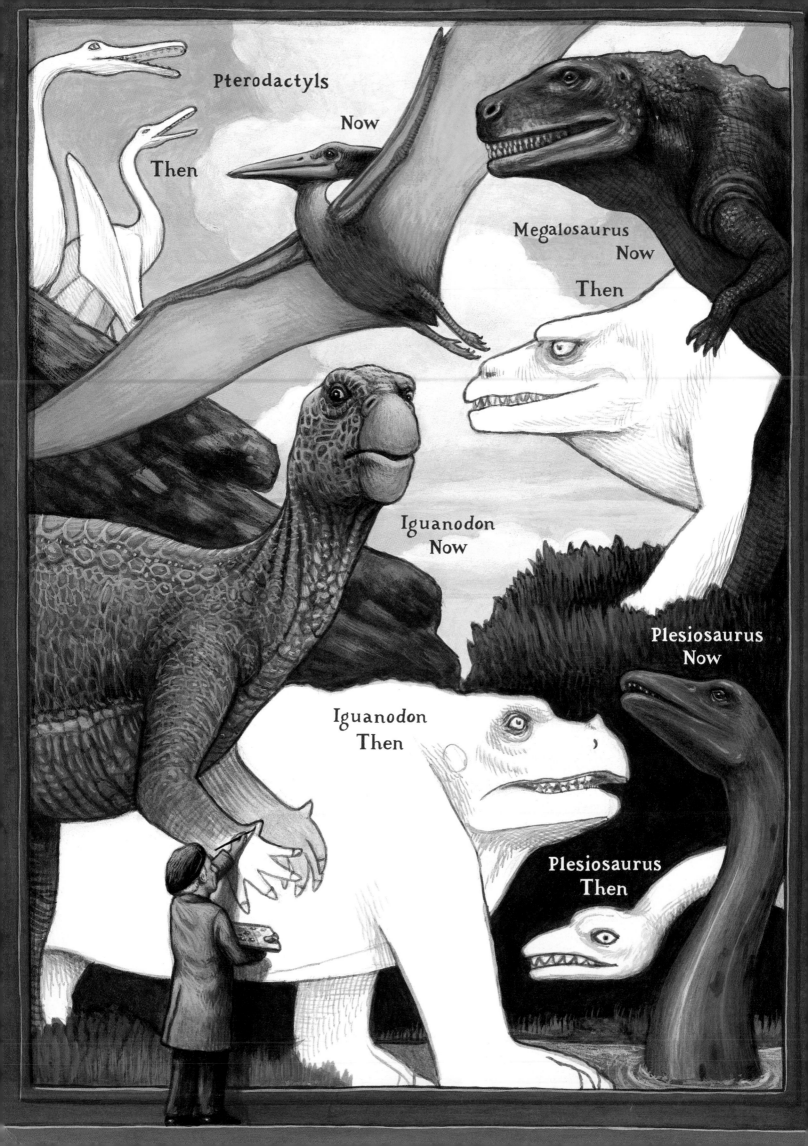

Bill of Fare

OF A DINNER GIVEN AT THE

CRYSTAL PALACE,

BY MR. WATERHOUSE HAWKINS

TO PROFESSOR OWEN AND TWENTY GENTLEMEN,

On SATURDAY, DECEMBER 31st, 1853,

IN THE MOULD OF

THE IGUANODON.

Soups.

Mock Turtle.   Jullien.   Hare.

Fish.

Cod and Oyster Sauce.   Fillets of Whiting.   Turbot à l'Hollandise.

Removes.

Roast Turkey.   Ham.   Raised Pigeon Pie.
Boiled Chicken and Celery Sauce.

Entrées.

Cotelette de Mouton aux Tomâtes.   Currie de Lapereau àu Riz.
Salmi de Perdrix.   Mayonnaise de Filêts de Sols.

Game.

Pheasants.   Woodcocks.   Snipes.

Sweets.

Madeira Jelly.   Orange Jelly.   Bavaroise
Charlotte de Russe.   French Pastry.   Nougat à la Chantilly.
Buisson de Meringue aux Confiteur.

Dessert.

Grapes.   Apples.   Pears.   Almonds and Raisins.   French Plums.
Pines.   Filberts.   Walnuts, &c. &c.

Wines.

Sherry.   Madeira.   Port.   Moselle.   Claret.

CHARLES HEGINBOTHOM,   AND EUROPEAN,
ANERLEY TAVERN,   MANSION HOUSE STREET.